In Despair, I Called Out to the Lord

A FARMER'S STORY OF THE POWER OF PRAYER

John Hookstead

TRILOGY CHRISTIAN PUBLISHERS

TUSTIN, CA

TRILOGY

Trilogy Christian Publishers
A Wholly Owned Subsidary of Trinity Broadcasting Network
2442 Michelle Drive
Tustin, CA 92780

IN DESPAIR, I CALLED OUT TO THE LORD: A Farmer's Story of the Power of Prayer

For information about special discounts for bulk purchases, please contact Trilogy Christian Publishing.

Manufactured in the United States of America

10 9 8 7 6 5 4 3 2 1

Library of Congress Cataloging-in-Publication Data is available.

ISBN: 978-1-68556-294-6

E-ISBN: 978-1-68556-295-3

Dedicated to Mom and Dad

Acknowledgements

For the Christian, thanking God for His help in our lives has been done and redone—sometimes to the point of sounding robotic. Like pushing the play and rewind buttons on a tape recorder repeatedly, the significance of a phrase can lose all meaning. Yet, in fact, there would be no reason to recount the events of our lives if not for God. His love and mercy make every joy greater and every heartbreak not only survivable, but wonderfully and knowingly just, right, and true. And so, yes, at the risk of sounding redundant, I will give God my gratitude and praise, for I know that all that is worthy originates and springs forth from Him.

Luke 10:27
Jesus answered, "Love the Lord your God
with all your heart and with all your soul and
with all your strength and with all your mind;
and love your neighbor as yourself."

In addition to God, I would like to thank my wife Kelly, my son Ethan, my mother and father, my caregivers, and the countless well-wishers whose prayers supported me in my hour of need.

To my wife, for her steadfast commitment to our marriage. To Ethan, for the big bear hugs whenever I needed one, and for growing up fast. And to both of them, for their faithful acceptance of the way our lives together underwent a sudden and dramatic change. To my parents, for making the sacrifices in their lives to be what a mother and father were designed to be. To my caregivers, for their skill and dedication. Then, finally, to all the unnamed well-wishers, both family and friends, that if formed in a line could reach and wind its way around the back forty, and who by the extension of their grace "loved their neighbor as themselves."

Foreword

John's story awoke in me two basic truths—truths that can too often be taken for granted through a sort of spiritual malaise. First, that Jesus is our Lord and Savior. He paid the penalty for our sins on the cross so that, if we repent and receive Him, death is conquered—let alone the troubles of this world. That is an indescribable peace. The second is that we are close to God through a *personal relationship* with Jesus.

I was reminded of the second truth when I read that John had "never known a more wonderful feeling" during his moment of tragedy. While I will never be able to relate to his experience, I do believe that, as a Christian, I know the "wonderful feeling" that he was referring to. In fact, this part of the book—God's strong presence during the tragedy—unexpectedly opened in me a flood of memories. Memories of God's unquestionable presence in my life as a youth. And by the time I got to page three, I knew that I had been missing it.

This planted in me a new seed and an urge to draw close to Him, knowing that He would then draw close to me (James 4:8). This leads me back to that second truth: that I know God through a personal relationship with Jesus—not through all the Bible verses I understand (which I must), or the church services I attend (which I should), or even my efforts to be a godly husband and father (which He commands), but rather by desiring a closeness with God through His Son and valuing that above all else.

And why? Because I am compelled by His great love for me (2 Cor. 5:14). A love that died for me. The same love that surrounded John with an unspeakable peace during what should have been the worst moment of his life. That is who our God is. The God who spoke the universe into existence with His Word is the same God who cast all the sin of mankind onto His perfect Son, Jesus, in order to save... me. Why? Because He loves me. That is astonishing, and I will never fully understand it. But I'll always believe it. John's story reminded me of it afresh. John will never know the full work of God during his life this side of heaven. But now he knows, as do you, just one small piece of it: a proper, loving jolt for me to desire and pursue a closer relationship with my Savior. In this way, God did a work in me through His servant, John.

You'll discover numerous other ways that God's hand worked in John's life and the lives of those close to him during this time. I pray that these pages will touch your heart in some area that God has designed especially for you. I pray that you'll be encouraged, as I have been, to look to the One who created us, loves us, saved us, and seeks us even now. You will "never know a more wonderful feeling."

Sam Fettig
Accomplished Musician, Music Teacher, and Friend

Contents

PSALM 23

The Lord is my Shepherd, I shall not be in want.
He makes me lie down in green pastures,
He leads me beside quiet waters,
He restores my soul.
He guides me in paths of righteousness
for His name's sake.

Even though I walk through the valley of the shadow of
death,
I will fear no evil,
for you are with me;
your rod and your staff,
they comfort me.

You prepare a table before me
in the presence of my enemies.
You anoint my head with oil;
my cup overflows.
Surely goodness and love will follow me
all the days of my life,
and I will dwell in the house of the Lord
forever.

Introduction

The pages within contain the story of injuries that I sustained in a farming accident in the autumn of 2019 and speak to the way in which God came to my aid. It is a story less about survival and loss, and more about faith and the power of prayer. It can be said that the events of this story are not about a faith found, but of the good fortune in having one's faith confirmed. My good spirits and quick—though not painless—recovery are by the grace of God. My recollection of the accident itself is very clear. I can't help but know that this is by God's design. Unlike many believers, I didn't have a proclivity for being wordy or vocal in my prayers. During this event, that would change. The Holy Spirit would fill my mind and open my mouth with words that comforted not only me, but also those involved in my care, recovery, and beyond. Having God to call upon in prayer turned tragedy into triumph, and I have felt the Holy Spirit urging me to recount the events of this fateful day, and the days that followed, to all who are willing to listen. I feel that God the Father has guided my pen. May this story bring glory to God and praise to His Son, Jesus the Christ. (1)

(1) **Matthew 11:15**
"Whoever has ears, let them hear."

PART ONE

The Accident

Proverbs 3:6
In all your ways submit to him, and he will
make your paths straight.

Checking on the cattle was always the first task of the morning. This day was no exception. Finding nothing out of the ordinary, I hurried through the feeding chores, grabbed some supplies, and put on a winter coat as a buffer against the cold breeze the cab-less tractor was sure to produce on the short drive up the road. I entered through the gateway of the cornfield a few minutes later to continue the time-honored tradition of the harvest (a season all too familiar to me, having lived my entire life on a farm).

It was cold, sunny, and approaching 11:00 on this Monday morning in late October. I attached the tractor to the hitch of the corn picker and did some routine maintenance, before starting the corn picker at an idle to check the function of a drive chain that I had repaired and reinstalled late in the afternoon the day before. Everything was working well, but I thought it best to relubricate the chain, using oil I had brought for this purpose. In doing so, I reached closer with my left arm than need be, and in that fraction of a second of not respecting the unyielding power of machinery parts in motion, the sleeve of my coat caught on a cog on a gear of the rotating driveshaft.

I pulled back with the amount of force only fear and adrenalin could elicit as my hand, and then my arm, began wrapping around the shaft like a string being wrapped around a finger. Making an effort as though it could be my last, I was still unable to free myself. As I was losing the battle to pull away, I repeatedly raked at my coat zipper in the hope that I could unzip and slip out of it. When this failed, I braced myself with my right arm and left knee against the frame of the corn picker and called out "No! No! No!" Then I began to pray the 23rd Psalm, at which point my fear immediately turned to peace. I was completely unafraid and filled with the "knowing" that my Lord and Savior, through the Holy Spirit, had His arms securely around me. (2) I became calm in body and deliberate in thought. I have never known a more wonderful feeling.

(2) John 14:16

"And I will ask the Father, and he will give you another advocate to help you and be with you forever."

While my arm continued to wrap around the shaft, I prayed that the sleeve of my coat would tear away and my arm would come apart; otherwise, I would be further drawn into the revolving mechanism. To what end, only God knows. First my hand, though unknown to me at the time, had severed at the wrist, and then—eventually, though I couldn't say how much later—the sleeve tore away, taking with it a length of my arm just above the elbow. I fell backward onto the ground and lay there with a feeling of comfort and security and the "knowing" that I wasn't alone. The Lord's reassuring embrace had me wanting to stay with Him. Forever.

My next memory is of Jesus saying, "No, not now." Not with words I could hear, but with His presence I could feel. I felt no harshness in his response. Only longing. But at no time did I have any sense of abandonment. Quite the contrary. The peace and calm only expanded. Then, after this gentle refusal of my request to stay with Him, the dilemma I faced encircled me again. The immediate properties of this life—the sound of the tractor and picker, the soil beneath me, the corn stalks to my right and left, the excruciating pain in my neck, and the awareness that my left arm was gone—all came rushing back into focus.

At this point, what was left of my arm didn't hurt a lot, but my neck burned with pain. My first idea to get help was to use my cell phone. I tried repeatedly, but my right hand and arm would not function well enough to get my phone out of my jeans pocket. I knew instinctively that whatever was plaguing my right arm emanated from the pain in my neck (it would later be revealed that I had broken and dislocated vertebrae starting at C6 through T1, which caused a spinal cord injury). Finding myself unable to move, the question now became what to do. I had to make a decision.

My parents live in the woods, a little less than two-tenths of a mile away from where I lay on the ground. The still-running tractor and picker were parked between myself and their house. Though I was close to the road, I was quite certain that the dense foliage that separated the road from the field would make it impossible for passersby to notice me. Being unable to get my phone, and believing that no one would see me, left me with only one slim possibility to be discovered. I would need to call for help in the hope that my parents would hear me.

Mom happened to be in the garage (hindsight tells me it was around 11:45 a.m.), throwing away a glass jar into the recycling. She would later say it was something she had intended to discard for a long time. Thankfully, this was the day and time she chose to do so. Mom heard my call for help and immediately got in her car and came to the field. With all the things that had to line up for Mom to hear me—her placement in the garage,

4

my strength or lack thereof to yell, the noise of the machinery, and the distance between us—all make it truly amazing that Mom heard me.

When Mom arrived in the field, I could not see her car but sensed that someone had come. Mom got out of the car and came to me, and cupped my face in her hands and said, "John, I'm here." She kept her cool, but being almost eighty-four, she felt ill-equipped to help lift me, so she opened the backseat door, and speaking to me like I was ten, sternly said, "John, get into this car right now."

Mom would later recount the struggle I had getting into her car. She described it as a grueling effort, relating that I pushed my way along the ground on my back toward the car door by using my legs and the heels of my shoes. Then, having arrived at the door and asking for her help, I inched my shoulders and back up against the door frame, and eventually the seat, where I rested a moment. Then, finally, with one last effort, I propelled myself into the car.

This is what Mom saw, but what I felt was entirely different. Taking into account my blood loss and broken neck, a struggle it would have been if not for the Lord. For I know that Jesus put me in Mom's car—whether He lifted me with His arms or gave me the strength to maneuver, I couldn't say. What I do know is that I was unable to sit up or get to my knees, much less stand.

With what seemed like little effort on my part, I suddenly found myself in the back of Mom's car. (3)

(3) **Psalm 34:7**
The angel of the Lord encamps around those
who fear him, and he delivers them.

So, with her youngest son lying across the back seat with a broken neck and left arm torn off, Mom closed the door, turned the car around, and steered through the gateway onto the road. Few of us will ever know what sixty-four years of committed marriage looks like, but on this day, I had an unobstructed view, and a beautiful view it was. As we left the field, Mom said, "I've got to go tell your father what's happening, so he won't worry and wonder where I am." What an amazing display of devotion. (4) I, though, insisted that she go immediately, or I may bleed out. With that frightening thought, Mom headed directly to Fort Atkinson.

(4) **Proverbs 31:10**
A wife of noble character who can find? She
is worth far more than rubies.

Fort Atkinson is the nearest town in our area equipped with a hospital. With clear sailing, it's about twenty minutes away from the field in which Mom found me. Clear sailing is exactly what Mom encountered on our dash to the ER. The traffic was sparse—both on the country roads and on the city streets. And the three traffic lights that Mom needed to negotiate were all on green. I encouraged Mom in her driving, asserting my notion that, given my condition, a car accident would only add to our problem. But of course, Mom kept her composure, and my words of concern weren't really necessary. My heart sank as I apologized to her for having to see one of her children in this condition, and I expressed, again, that I might bleed out and that I might not make it. She assured me that that wasn't the case, from what she could see, and said I should continue to pray. My trust in Mom's assessment was complete and without reservation—a mother's reassurance is a wonderful blessing. As I returned to prayer, I truly knew I was being heard. God, the Father, was listening. (5)

(5) Psalm 18:6

In my distress I called to the Lord; I cried to
my God for help. From His temple
he heard my voice; my cry came before him,
into his ears.

Mom pulled up to the ER's sliding-glass doors and ran inside to get help. Two young women hurried out with a wheelchair. I can only imagine what they were thinking when Mom opened the car door. There seemed to be a second of indecision on how to get me out of the car. I said to Mom, "I can't walk." Mom's response was typical when she said, "Oh yes, you can!" It was more of an order than a statement. So, with a great deal of effort on everyone's part, I came to a seated position, swung my legs out, stood up, turned, and collapsed into the waiting wheelchair. The nurses quickly whisked me away, down a hallway and into a room, and I was placed on a table.

My prayers continued as a flurry of activity started up around me. My neck had been the most painful part of this ordeal so far, and my corn picker amputation didn't seem to hurt that badly, but that was about to change. With my arrival at the ER, the pain in what remained of my left arm took center stage. It's a pain I've never really been able to describe. In truth, it was almost beyond my endurance. I was making petitions to God and everyone in that room. I was calling for help and asking for Kelly, my wife. I was also making a prayerful request to God to give my caregivers strength and to help them draw on their knowledge.

With my next breath, I talked to God the Father. I told Him I was sorry—sorry I had been unable or unwilling to forgive others the way He has forgiven me. (6,7) It was an act of contrition, from the depths of my soul, as I continued to implore that someone call my wife. I was being assured that she was on her way as I was asking for them to call my pastor. They said they would, but they didn't know his number (and why would they?). I had never committed my pastor's number to memory, but astonishingly, I was able to recite it to them.

(6) **Mark 11:25**
"And when you stand praying, if you hold
anything against anyone,
forgive them, so that your Father in heaven
may forgive you your sins."

(7) **Daniel 9:9**
The Lord our God is merciful and forgiving,
even though we have rebelled against him.

Next, a doctor placed a tourniquet on my left arm. Then a nurse anesthetist put a nerve block in my left shoulder. This greatly reduced the pain, and I could once again envision life.

With the pain under control, I began to focus on other concerns. When I was lying on the ground in the field, I was unable to get my phone out of my pocket. This came to mind in the ER, and so I asked them, "Can somebody tell me what's wrong with my right arm?" Of course, at this point, they didn't know. I also asked how much of my left arm could be saved. More specifically, the question was, "Will I keep my shoulder?" I became more and more insistent that I have an answer to this question. My insistence wasn't that of frustration or anger, but more of an intense and deep need to know what remained of my arm. With the answer not forthcoming, my agitation grew.

In hindsight, I recognize that the ER personnel probably couldn't give me a definitive answer, and any response could only be their best guess. They also may have thought that no answer was better than the wrong one, and so I continued to ask over and over.

Other than my wife's, I have no lasting memory of anyone's voice while I lay on that table—except for one. The words I heard were like that of an angel, but the nurse who spoke them was as mortal as anyone in that room. She came close and said, "Yes, I think you'll keep your shoulder." With that, my restlessness faded away, and I felt a great peace come over me. Her voice was the most beautiful sound. It was of this world, but at the same time, not of this world. I knew she was God's messenger. (8)

(8) **Luke 4:10**
"For it is written: 'He will command
His angels concerning you to guard you
carefully.'"

My next memory is vivid. It is that of Pastor Dave. The staff had been able to reach him using the number I had given them. He stood next to me. If he said anything to me, I don't recall, but it was a great comfort having him there. He is a man of God who holds himself in quiet dignity and projects a simple, honest faith—just the sort of person you want to come alongside when your need is great.

Soon after that, Kelly arrived. Mom had gone home and called Kelly's workplace. She told her I had had a serious accident, and that I was at the ER in Fort Atkinson. She didn't describe my injuries to Kelly, but ended her call with the words "He's alive." In the coming days and weeks, I've often thought about that. What a dreadful thing Kelly had to hear, and to speculate the meaning of, as she got in her car and drove the fifteen-plus minutes to the hospital.

My feeling of relief upon Kelly's arrival was enormous. I felt her presence in the room before she came near. When she approached, I felt the weight of her hand as she placed it on my left shoulder. I expressed to her that I was sorry for letting this happen to us, and that I knew this would change everything for us as a family. She said it would be okay, and not to worry about that right now. I, surprisingly, cannot remember seeing her face, but the words she spoke and the familiar and soothing way in which she said them painted a picture of her for me. I was so exhausted and struggling to stay with her in that moment, but the sound of her voice had me drifting off into a very peaceful state. And, while I rested, I was wheeled to the helicopter that would fly me to the University of Wisconsin Hospital in Madison.

My memory of the flight is limited. I had two attendants, and of course, I was sedated. Mostly, I just remember listening to the rotors of the helicopter going round-and-round. This was my first flight of any kind. Being on the farm, and a homebody besides, I'd never before had need, or occasion, to fly. We landed at the hospital in Madison—a flight, I'm told, that took about eighteen minutes. I recall the feeling of "touch-down," and the bumpiness of the sidewalk when being taken from the helicopter pad into the hospital, but that's where my memory of the first part of this journey ends.

PART TWO

The Hospital

My recollection of the accident and the events at the Fort Atkinson ER are very clear, and have been easily recalled, but my memory of the first three days in Madison... not so much. In fact, it doesn't exist. I'm glad there are others to help fill in the blanks. I was admitted for surgery immediately. That was at about 1:30 p.m. on Monday. It wouldn't be until Thursday morning, when I was taken off the ventilator and brought out of sedation, that my memory of events would begin again. Although my memory would be temporarily interrupted with the need for surgery, I learned later that I prayed right up until I was fully anesthetized.

The fact that I continued to pray was discovered, I believe, by happenstance. Still, some think it was no coincidence. My niece is a massage therapist. Days after my arrival in Madison, she had an appointment to give a massage to a woman who turned out to be an ER nurse at the UW. My niece told her that her uncle had recently had a farm accident and was currently at the UW Hospital. From the description of my injuries, the woman made the connection. She had been one of many that had attended to me in surgery. She told my niece, "Your uncle prayed aloud until he was put under for surgery." (9) What an amazing realization: above all else, I was petitioning the Holy Spirit and was drawing comfort from my Savior. I may have been placed into the hands of different doctors, at a different hospital, but it was Jesus who was with me from the beginning, and He would decide the outcome.

(9) **Jeremiah 29:12**
"Then you will call on me and come and pray
to me, and I will listen to you."

My caregivers discovered early on that there really was no hope of reattaching my left arm. Even if it could have been retrieved in time from the field, the way it was crushed and torn away would certainly have left it beyond repair. With that being the case, the surgeons would turn their attention on what to tackle first—my arm, or my neck? It was eventually decided that they would conduct some of the procedures simultaneously. The orthopedic team would work on my arm, while the spinal surgeon and his team would repair my neck.

First, my arm was thoroughly cleaned and scrubbed of the grease and oil that the chain had ground into it, which was considerable. Next, they would close the wound. Thankfully, there was a flap of skin and muscle yet hanging from my left upper arm that would serve this purpose well. At the same time, the spinal team worked to stabilize the dislocated vertebrae. They first went through the front of my neck to affix a plate, with screws, to the injured vertebrae. They also discovered that the back of the dislocated vertebrae had crumbled and broken away. It was then that they realized they would have to turn me over to insert rods and more screws to more completely stabilize the area. Lastly, they would take bone from my hip and lay it on and over the affected vertebrae. The technique involved is to connect, or fuse, the vertebrae directly above and below the broken one, making the three function as one. The biggest problem they encountered was uncontrolled bleeding. They had to stop and pack the area in ice to aid in coagulation. In all, I was given thirteen units of blood (fluid), which I am told is a lot. At some point, with the bleeding controlled, they finished repairing the vertebrae.

The surgical team began their decision making on how best to help me at around 1:30 that Monday afternoon. They completed the surgery at about 12:15 a.m. Tuesday morning, making it a total of approximately eleven hours from start to finish. From surgery, I was moved to the Trauma Life Support Center (TLC), where

I would remain sedated for three days. Describing the surgical team's work in layman's terms makes it all sound so simple, but I'm sure it wasn't. And I'm grateful to God for placing me in their skilled hands.

Through it all, Kelly, my son, my sister and her husband, my niece, and a friend of Kelly's had gathered together at the UW Hospital and were all participating in the hardest part of all—the waiting.

The friend, named Lori, had driven Kelly to Madison. They had met one another in church years before. It was in preparation for a mission trip to Lithuania that their friendship had blossomed. Kelly knew that Lori worked at the hospital where I was taken to first and inquired as to whether Lori was at work that day. It was determined that she was, and someone sent word for her to come to the ER. I had just been placed on the helicopter, but Kelly was not allowed to accompany me and would need to drive to Madison on her own. Kelly didn't feel up to the task of making that drive alone, so she asked Lori to drive. Lori got permission to leave work early, and off they went to meet me at the UW Hospital.

Lori is a thoughtful and strong woman—not prone to exaggeration or uncontrolled emotion. She is a lady of many gifts and talents. She is a long-time Christian—well-versed in the truth of our Savior's Word. (10) She was just the person who needed to be with my Kelly during that forty-five-minute drive. It was good that Kelly wouldn't be alone to face all of the unknowns about what was next for her husband. I am so thankful to the Lord for knowing that, on this day, my family's need would be great, and for having Lori there to shoulder some of the burden.

(10) **Proverbs 31:26**
She speaks with wisdom, and faithful instruction is on her tongue.

My amputated arm was scheduled to be examined and cleaned on Tuesday, but was rescheduled for Wednesday, because other patients had arrived at the UW Hospital with more urgent needs. I was brought out of sedation on Thursday morning, with Kelly at my bedside. I opened my eyes and began to become fully aware of my surroundings. There were devices designed to monitor my vital signs. There was the glass door and curtain that provided this room, in the TLC, privacy. There was a nurse attending me who seemed to be wearing his shoes out, going back and forth from one job to another. The room was well-lit, but the light was soft and easy on my eyes. This small area was packed with objects that made this space what it was meant to be—a place to recover. I could have been distracted by any one of the room's amenities, but the truth is, all I could see was Kelly. She held my right hand tight. I tried to squeeze back but, for the time being, was unable. My left arm was gone, and my partially paralyzed right hand lay limp in hers. I'm sure we talked a little, but I couldn't say what about. What mattered most was that I was back with her after being away for three days. For she is like a warm spring day on which my love for her is in continuous bloom. (11) In a short while, I found myself falling back to sleep. Kelly encouraged me to rest, and as I drifted off, I was left to wonder how I would ever hold her again as I had before.

(11) **Song of Songs 4:1**
How beautiful you are, my darling!
Oh, how beautiful!

While the work of my recovery had just begun, the needs of our farm were ongoing. Farm accidents of this magnitude, as a tradition, bring out a lot of support. In our case, it was no different. So, while Kelly's attention remained focused on my recovery, there would be a huge outpouring of help from family, friends, and neighbors.

My wife Kelly and I live with our son on a small farm in southeastern Wisconsin. It's very small by today's standards. We raise Black Angus beef cattle to be sold on the open market, and we offer beef for people's home freezers. At a time when farmers have had to leave the land for financial reasons, we have been able to survive. The ways in which we've found to remain doing what we love are all too common. Beginning with my parents' penchant for planning, tending to the needs of the farm seven days a week, a milk-trucking business I used to own, and Kelly's job as a pharmacy technician at a local pharmacy are all factors that have contributed to our modest success. I have often quipped that I don't love anything but the Lord and the land. The land usually being a distant second. The land has always provided me with my every need—starting with useful and purposeful work, a place to admire and be amazed by nature, a place to experience all four seasons, and a feeling of accomplishment and satisfaction of being there from when the seeds were planted in the spring to when the crop was harvested in the fall. I have been blessed to have a wife who has understood my sometimes-all-consuming love for the land, and a Savior in Jesus who has interceded on my behalf when my love for the land came a little too close to surpassing my love for my Heavenly Father.

Of course, all of this sentiment about the land doesn't mean half as much as the people who came to help when we needed them most. Because when it comes to livestock, no matter what happens, the world does not stop. The cattle need to be fed and watered every day, regardless of the situation. Without being asked, family and friends came daily and did the feeding chores for the month I was hospitalized. They would also harvest the corn. They willingly disrupted their lives so I could peacefully, and without worry concentrate solely on recovery. It was a gift they gave freely. (12) It's the kind of thing one just could never repay. Ours was a scenario that the saying "Don't pay it back; pay it forward" was made for.

(12) **Matthew 10:8**
Freely you have received; freely give.

Still, there was one decision that had to be made: what to do with the cattle in the long term? In the short term, they were being cared for by my sister, my son Ethan, and other family members. But this couldn't go on indefinitely. Above all else, farming is a hands-on occupation. If ever I was to return to farming in the capacity that I once enjoyed, all of the following would need to be attended to: repairing fences, maintaining machinery, handling and moving cattle, the upkeep of the farm buildings, not to mention planting and harvesting. In my current condition, I couldn't imagine accomplishing any one of these tasks, let alone all of them. I had lost my left arm, and there was some paralysis of my right.

On the surface, it looks like an easy call, a "no-brainer," as it's said. Sell the cattle. Right. But wait—stop to consider a number of factors. Farming is a way of life. There's never a dull moment. You never have to look too far for something interesting to do. You never have to yearn for a weekend getaway when you're doing what you love every day. There's also the independence of thought and action. Insert here the oft-repeated line from a Frank Sinatra song, "I did it my way." This phrase certainly applies.

Also, Ethan was almost twelve. His interest in the cattle, crops, and the land was growing. What would his teenage years look like without the duty and responsibility of caring for the animals? What would we do as a family without this routine? Of course, the aforementioned concerns are all about pride and worry. (13) They're not about fully trusting God and seeking His guidance, and knowing that He would have an answer for us in due time. (14) So, given that understanding and the permanence of my injuries, we made the decision to first, remove the cattle from our farm as timely as possible, and second, market them at a later date. My brother Chris would be instrumental in this process.

(13) James 4:6
But he gives us more grace. That is why Scripture says: "God opposes the proud but shows favor to the humble."

(14) **Joshua 1:9**

"Have I not commanded you? Be strong
and courageous. Do not be afraid; do not be
discouraged, for the Lord your God will be
with you wherever you go."

Chris was born in 1958. I was born in 1966. That makes
him eight years my elder. For closeness among siblings, this is
usually a span in years which is hard to bridge. Just consider
the different life stages we were always in. When I was one, he
was nine and transitioning from playing to helping Dad on the
farm. When I was five, Chris was a young adult of thirteen,
already foreseeing chores that needed to be done. When I was
eight, he was of legal driving age. Finally, when I was ten and
finding myself transitioning from playing "farm" in the sand
box to actually being helpful on Dad's farm, he had graduated
from high school and was on his own. So, the things we had in
common were few. Though there was one thing that worked to
our advantage. We were separated enough in years to elimi-
nate sibling rivalry and the competition that usually comes
with it.

He was out of the house and as I recall, had different jobs,
but it wouldn't be long before he would begin a farm operation
of his own. Beginning at age ten, I would take every opportu-
nity to join him in whatever he was doing. It wasn't all that
often, because of course, Dad had plenty for me to do at home.

Consequently, our time together was somewhat limited, but it wasn't for lack of trying on my part. The time I did get to spend with him wasn't exactly the picturesque version of older brother/younger brother relationships. He didn't take me fishing or to ball games, which are fine activities, but too often someone else's preconceived idea of fun. No, we didn't do those things, but for me, the things we did were pure adventure. Chris was larger than life and not afraid of anything. He had a spirit and an energy that couldn't be matched. Whenever he needed a little help (emphasis on little), I was quick to volunteer. If Dad could spare me, off we would go in his pick-up. Speeding away to some unknown adventure had me feeling like I had just won the lottery. Whether it was to clean calf pens, bale hay, move cattle, prepare a piece of ground for planting, or simply to help him bring something home that he had purchased at an auction, it didn't matter—I was right where I wanted to be. And at the end of the day, he would treat me to a McDonald's hamburger and fries—which was a big deal, because unlike kids today, I didn't grow up seeing the inside of very many restaurants. Then he would take me home. Having been gone all day, I'd arrive ready for bed and feeling like I'd just accomplished some sort of secret mission. Such is the mind of a ten-year-old.

When I reached the ages of thirteen and fourteen, I would sometimes spend several days and nights at his farm. Chris needed few creature comforts, so to describe the time spent with him as "roughing it" would be an understatement. I didn't go there to watch TV or play video games or to stare at a smart-

phone; I was there to be helpful. The days started at sunup and ended at nightfall. In the summertime, that usually meant about fourteen to fifteen hours. While in his charge, I learned to appreciate a sunrise and the grandeur of sleeping on an old, lumpy couch at day's end, having just enough energy to take off my boots before I fell onto it. Chris always kept me well-fed, but I always had the feeling that if I wasn't there, he wouldn't stop for meals. I'd like to think I held my own, but if I didn't, it wasn't for lack of desire. It's just that trying to keep up with Chris was a fool's errand. His passion and drive were unconquerable. And so, I had a bird's-eye view of a remarkable young man of about twenty-three years old. I learned a lot about not giving up. That lesson has served me well many times, before and since my accident.

Chris's farm operation and other responsibilities have grown since those early days. Consequently, for him, time, like any other commodity, has to be well-managed. Over the course of the next few weeks following my accident, he would come and load our cattle onto a trailer a few at a time and take them to one of his properties, where they would be fed and watered. He also handled the marketing of them. Through the years, I have often asked Chris for advice. I could never have known I would need him for something of this magnitude. I may not have known, but fortunately, God surely did. (15)

(15) **Proverbs 17:17**

A friend loves at all times, and a brother is
born for a time of adversity.

Thursday passed mostly uneventfully. I was very
groggy, and my awareness of the goings-on around me
were foggy, at best. I listened to the beeping of the vari-
ous machines monitoring my vital signs. Occasionally,
I would hear Kelly talking with my nurse. Later in the
day, though, the world started to come more into focus.
At some point in the early afternoon, a speech therapist came to see me in the TLC. After we exchanged
pleasantries, she came to the reason for her visit. One
of my attending physicians had ordered something
called a swallow test. She said that since the surgery to
repair the broken vertebrae had gone through the front
of my neck as well as the back, the swallow reflex was
brought into question. She described the procedure she
would need to perform in detail, as was the case whenever anything was prescribed for me. She told me that
I would be given a spoonful of solution to swallow, and
as I did so, an x-ray would be taken of my throat. She
said that in a normal swallow reflex, a person's airway
closes and virtually simultaneously, the passageway to
the stomach opens. She said this was an involuntary reflex—meaning a person doesn't have to think about it,

it just happens. What had to be discovered was whether that reflex was functioning properly. If it wasn't, I could aspirate (if food or drink failed to go to my stomach, but rather entered my airway instead). When she had finished, she asked if I understood, and would I be up for this test? I said, "Sure," and then I added, "especially since I'm in no position to say no." Evidently the pain medication still had me feeling good enough that I was able to make this small attempt at humor.

It wasn't long after the speech therapist left that my nurse came with a wheelchair to take me for the test. My nurse placed a gait belt around me so he could better lift and guide me into the wheelchair. I never went any-where for the month I spent in the UW Hospital system without that belt. So, with a lot of help from both the nurse and Kelly, I got into the chair, and off we went, with the IV cart and monitor in tow. Believe it or not, I was having quite a nice time being whooshed down hallways, through doors, and then down the elevator. I wouldn't have been having so much fun if I had known the end result of this journey.

We arrived at the speech therapist's office with her and an assistant waiting for us. She had been nicely dressed when she visited me in my room, but now she had a stain-covered smock on over her clothes. This should have been a tip-off about how things might go, yet I didn't have a clue.

She welcomed me and helped me stand. Then she tied an x-ray blanket on me. She positioned me in front of an x-ray machine, and with her holding the spoon, I swallowed a big spoonful of a chalky, white substance. When I did so, a great portion of this liquid raced directly into my airway. I choked and gasped for air for what seemed like well over a minute. Through water-filled eyes, I glanced over at the speech therapist. She was calm and collected and seemed quite confident that I would survive, even if I wasn't so sure. Even though she didn't seem concerned, her assistant's facial expression was one of great sympathy. When I regained my composure, she said that the test had been conclusive, and as she had suspected, I had an issue with swallowing. She also said that, given the surgery I'd had, the result of the test was not unexpected. The speech therapist said that she would give the recommendation for my diet to the nutritionist. With that said, Kelly and my nurse took me back to the TLC. To be sure, I wasn't having quite as nice of a time on the return trip and was thinking the whole way back of that old saying of how "the cure might be worse than the condition." The not-so-nice things I thought about the therapist and this test made me wish that God couldn't know my thoughts. Thankfully, I would have an opportunity to ask her forgiveness for the things I had thought about her before I was released.

Late in the afternoon, Pastor Dave and his wife paid me a visit. I was glad to see them, and I know Kelly was too. Seeing their faces was another one of those early reminders that I was still among the living, and that life would, in one way or another, continue. I was weak in body, but strong in desire to tell them, including Kelly, what the Holy Spirit had done for me. More than anything, I wanted them to know that when I called on our Savior in prayer, He was right there, and I felt His arms securely around me. It's the story—the same story—that's been on my lips and in my heart since I reentered the world after being sedated for surgery. And in the coming days and weeks, I would share it with family, friends, caregivers, and fellow patients. (16)

(16) **Psalm 40:10**

I do not hide your righteousness in my heart;
I speak of your faithfulness and your saving help.
I do not conceal your love and your
faithfulness from the great assembly.

With the exception being the swallow test, the time ticked away quickly and easily Thursday afternoon. That began to change in the late evening and into early Friday morning. The nerve block that had been so effective at the Fort Atkinson ER four days earlier had been removed in favor of other pain-relieving medications that were, in my case, less successful. Consequently, the pain in my amputation intensified. So much so that by 2:00 a.m., my pain threshold had been all but reached. I was exhausted and so was Kelly, who had been up with me all night. Often, answers to medical questions come slowly. Well, let me tell you that at 2:00 a.m., they come even slower.

Kelly first turned to our nurse. We discovered that the nurse really didn't have the authority to change my prescription, and there weren't a lot of physicians to call on at that hour of the night. After a lot of pleading by Kelly on my behalf, she was able to speak to the intern (which is a first-year resident). She was only able to offer us a form of over-the-counter, topical pain reliever. It didn't help very much. So, Kelly and I ended up spending an agonizing and sleepless night in the TLC.

Relief would come in the morning, when the attending physicians arrived at the hospital—namely, my anesthesiologist. He came to the TLC with his followers in tow. By followers, I mean the resident, the intern, and sometimes someone called a chief. The UW is a teaching hospital. So, when a doctor needs to come to your room, they bring with them doctors-in-training, and the doctor-in-training with the most years of experience usually performs the procedure. If they have difficulty, the full-fledged doctor takes over. In this case, my anesthesiologist came to reinsert the nerve block in my left shoulder, which had been inexplicably removed. He also decided to give me a pain medication intravenously that I could deliver myself once every ten minutes by use of a push button. It was programmed so it could never supply more than one dose every ten minutes. There was this protocol which stated that I (the patient) was the only person allowed to push the button. Well, this was impossible, because my right hand was barely functioning. So Kelly, or whoever was visiting, would clandestinely push the button for me. It was like we were saboteurs, or spies, or something along those lines. We all had a little fun breaking this rule that, given my condition, seemed rather absurd. It was the next little bit of humor brought to this serious situation.

As I said, my anesthesiologist arrived at my room in the morning. I was very tired but listened intently as he discussed the nerve block procedure with his underlings. The main task he told the resident was to "find the right place to insert the needle and then secure it at the proper depth." His subordinate asked, "What do I do if I put the needle in too far?" The doctor's answer was humorous, and a little sarcastic. He responded by saying, "Well, then, pull it out a bit." I found him very likeable, and he seemed like kind of a maverick, which suited me just fine. It wasn't long after they had completed their work that the pain began to lessen. Before they left, the anesthesiologist instructed me on the use of the pain pump and finished by saying, "Don't be a cowboy. Push the button before the pain becomes intolerable." I assured him that I would, and I added, "Fancying myself a cowboy is partially how I got into this mess!" This good doctor had a remarkable personality. I don't know his faith, or even if he had a religious conviction, but I believe he would be a tremendous force if he put his hands to work for the Lord. Either way, he's someone I won't soon forget.

Having been awake through the night, Friday morning found me very tired. Now that some of the issues with the pain medication had been addressed, I was better able to rest. Kelly's continued presence brought a sense of peace to a surprisingly noisy TLC. By mid-morning, I was out like a light. I awoke around noon to Kelly's tired but smiling face. Soon after I awoke, my sister, Jackie, arrived. It was then that Kelly would take her leave. It was hard to see her go, but there were things to attend to at home. She'd been with me in Madison since Monday. Ethan had been in the care of his aunt. Kelly and I decided it was time to get him back to some sort of normalcy. I told her that I loved her, and again, that I was sorry. She said she loved me too, and, "I don't want to hear any more apologies, and there was never any need for one in the first place." We prayed for her safe travel and my continued recovery. It was a simple prayer that got used a lot. (17) The words we used may not have been eloquent, but we knew God was listening, and of course, there are no style points awarded for flowery language. What mattered most was that we placed ourselves in God's hands and trusted that He was still in control. After a held hand and a kiss, off she went, but not before having a brief word with Jackie.

(17) Matthew 6:7

"And when you pray, do not keep on babbling
like pagans,
for they think they will be heard because of
their many words."

Jackie is the youngest of my seven siblings and eight years my junior. She has many God-given gifts, starting with the ability to speak her mind when the moment calls for it, which would be terrible if she wasn't right so often. She is a whirlwind of energy—one would be well-served to get out of the way and let it blow over. Her sense of humor is second to none, and she has a capacity for compassion that, at times, seems boundless. She can be stylish beyond recognition, but can get down and dirty when need be. And oh, did I fail to mention that she also sings like an angel? Yet the greatest among her virtues is the highly prized one of discernment, which our entire family has had the good fortune to draw upon.

Of course, before she was all of these things, she was just our little sister—the last born of eight. Possessed with the natu-

ral ability to annoy her sister, the closest to her in age, and to wrap her six brothers around her little finger—and you might say "bend us all to her will," for which we adored her all the more. As she grew, it became quite clear that the words "just" and "little" would have to be removed from the phrase "just our little sister," for as time went by, she became a force unto her own, worthy of an identity all her own. She would eventually become the glue that, at times, was needed to hold our family together. Her force of personality and great sense of justice were just what the doctor ordered.

Jackie learned early on how to dispense advice, and with age, learned when it was simply best to listen—two character traits that I'm sure came in handy as she married, raised children, and owned and operated her own hair salon. My sister has always put more into people than she's gotten in return. At least, I know that to be true in my case. She's been there for me on numerous occasions. I hesitate to compile a list for fear of leaving something out, though I would be remiss if I didn't mention the three that I'm most grateful for: the first was buying groceries and storing them away when I was too busy to do it myself; the second was decorating a Christmas tree for me when I was alone and unattached; and the third was arranging a very special event at my wedding. Those may not be Jackie's top three, especially given how many there have been, but they're the ones I remember with the greatest amount of love and admiration. A great sister can be an answer to a prayer.

So, it wasn't surprising that Mom's first call, after Kelly, was to Jackie. It's the same call I would have made had I been in Mom's position. Like so often before, in good times or bad, Jackie was called in for support. Knowing that I had been med-flighted to Madison, her first instinct was to see to the needs of Kelly and Ethan. She drove to the UW to be with them while I was in surgery.

Jackie's arrival that Friday afternoon helped to assuage my heavy-heartedness about Kelly's departure. I felt very secure with my sister assuming the watch. Not to take anything away from the nursing staff, but it was good to have someone there to advocate for me, especially in the early stages, when I was at my weakest. Obviously, my nurses couldn't be with me every minute of every hour, because they had other patients that needed attention. My right hand was, more or less, paralyzed, so I couldn't even push the nurses' call button. Later on, when I got a little stronger, they gave me a call button that I could activate by applying the weight of my forearm. Also, trying to reposition myself in bed proved to be quite impossible. Above all else, I needed help to get a drink of water. The pain medication had given me a severely dry mouth, so having someone there to swab my mouth or to assist me in getting a drink was critical.

Having my sister there felt very comfortable. It was a very déjà vu moment, because she had come to my aid at other trying times. Of course, they all paled in comparison to this time. As I recall, we chatted a little, and

I dutifully asked about how things were at home. She filled me in on all who were pitching in to help with the farm work. I must admit, it was a half-hearted inquiry. The actual physical trauma of the accident and the danger it posed to my life was several days behind me, and the haze of the sedation from surgery had fully lifted. Now I was faced with a harsh reality. It wasn't coming to the realization of my physical impairment that was bothering me. No, that wasn't it at all. For the Lord had shielded me from the depression, fear, and anxiety that often accompanies this kind of injury. (18)

(18) **Psalm 34:4**
I sought the Lord, and he answered me;
he delivered me from all my fears.

It was more about coming to the understanding that I was now back in the world. There were three elements to the equation: physical, mental, and emotional. Though physically broken, I could rely on the system of care designed to support my recovery. As for the mental part, I was prepared to meet head-on the big changes that were looming on the horizon. However, emotionally, I was still in that cornfield. The physical presence that I had felt of the Lord in that field was something that I was unwilling to give up. Furthermore, the peace I had with Him is beyond description. So, the prospect of returning to this life was not very enticing. Yet this was really a rebellious perception of what had happened. I had called upon my Savior to be with me when I was caught and unable to free myself. And He came. The peace I had felt at that moment was that of wanting to stay with Him, but He said, "No, not now." And so, He did not give me eternal rest. Not yet. What He did give me then, and what stays with me now, is a feeling a freedom, and with that, a "knowing" that only with Him can the chains of this world be thrown off. (19) My new-found ability to more fully trust and follow Jesus is a gift the Holy Spirit has provided. Not questioning God's desire and decision to keep me here in this life is part of that trusting and following.

(19) **Jeremiah 17:7-8**
"But blessed is the one who trusts in the
Lord, whose confidence is in him. They will
be like a tree planted by the water that sends
out its roots by the stream. It does not fear
when heat comes; its leaves are always green.
It has no worries in a year of drought and
never fails to bear fruit."

Medically speaking, I had come a long way since Monday afternoon. Having nearly lost my life on Monday to resting comfortably by Friday was no short distance to travel. But there was one pressing need that had to be addressed that Friday evening—nutrition. How to deliver it was the question. I hadn't eaten anything in five days. The fluids I was given kept me hydrated, but I really hadn't taken in any calories. And calories, I was to learn, were needed for healing. So, around 6:00 p.m., a doctor came to explain my options. Since I had failed the swallow test, it would be more accurate to say "option." For there really was only one thing to do. The insertion of a naso-gastric tube (NG-tube) or, as I referred to it, a feeding tube. He explained the procedure. A tube would be inserted through my nose, down my throat, and past my stomach, where it would ultimately come to rest in my small intestine. The doctor assured me that the procedure wasn't as bad as it sounded and that it should take only a couple of minutes. Once completed, I would receive, day and night, a nutrient solution until I could eat by mouth. It would also be used to deliver medicine.

As a matter of routine, the doctor asked for my thoughts on the subject. I said that I was really in no position to say no. There's that line again. It was something I said often in giving my consent. The doctor excused himself, saying he would be back in a little while to perform the procedure. I have to admit, it didn't sound very fun. Fortunately, the Lord had instilled in me if not a trust in, at least an acceptance of the process. The Holy Spirit supplied for me the remarkable ability to stop the need for coveting control of events. (20) For most of us, if not all, desiring control is paramount to our daily lives. It gives us a sense of security, albeit a false one. Of course, relinquishing our need for control to the Lord brings courage to events where only fear and anxiety might have presided, thus freeing us to act in accordance with God's will.

(20) **Matthew 26:39**
Going a little farther, he fell with his face to
the ground and prayed,
"My Father, if it is possible, may this cup be
taken from me.
Yet not as I will, but as You will."

When the doctor returned with his charges, he explained to me that my one job was to swallow and to continue to swallow after the NG-tube entered my throat from my nasal passage. That sounded simple enough. After I gave my permission to have the resident insert the tube, the procedure got underway. I detected some reluctance on her part, but nonetheless, she was determined to give it the old college try. While unpleasant, everything was going fine until the NG-tube began to enter my throat, at which point it triggered my gag reflex. Now, the unpleasantness turned into a few really distressing seconds, which seemed like minutes.

My discomfort seemed to rattle the confidence of the resident. To her credit, she pushed on, and soon the tube was through my stomach. All that remained was to insert it into my small intestine. After several failed attempts, she asked the doctor to take over. He said, "You're doing fine," and encouraged her to continue. After several more tries, she insisted that the doctor finish the procedure, exclaiming, "I think I'm hurting him." The doctor assumed control and finished up rather quickly. Everyone in the room seemed relieved that it was done. It turned out to be worse than the doctor had described, but not half as bad as one might imagine. My heart really went out to the resident. It can't be easy inflicting pain on someone, even if that pain is short-lived and necessary.

Saturday morning ushered in a big change. I was informed that I was moving up in the world, not only in status but also in location. My condition had improved enough to allow me to be moved out of the TLC to the general care on the fourth floor, where I would spend the next seven days. I would get a room with a view and a new set of nurses that were every bit as capable and compassionate as those in the TLC. I would also be monitored daily by what the UW called the Trauma Team, the same doctors I had in the TLC. The team consisted of more physicians and their subordinates than I care to count, coming and going at all hours of the day, but especially in the early morning. Their primary objective was to see to it that my care continued in a positive manner and to address any concerns I may have had.

By mid-morning, I was wheeled out of the TLC. I stayed in the same bed, which negated the need to be transferred to a gurney or wheelchair, making the process easier for everyone. The attendant pushed me out of the TLC and onto an elevator that would take me to the fourth floor. Following close behind was a wheeled cart carrying the IV and vital signs monitor, propelled by Jackie, who had stayed with me the night before. Given all the things that had to be unplugged or plugged in, adjusted, moved, or reset, I could only describe the process of moving as controlled chaos. Yet in good time, I was settled into my new surroundings, no worse for the wear. And the new nursing staff made me feel right at home.

The appeal of my new room quickly ran its course, and I was left with two focal points of thought. The first was my growing compulsion to tell everyone, from my caregivers to my visitors, what the Holy Spirit had done when I had called on Him in prayer. Of course, it was the fact that in my fear He had held me tight, lest I be alone in that field (21), and the "knowing" that He was with me, which brought calm and peace to an otherwise frightening situation. The second was the pain I was experiencing, even under medication. To be more specific: phantom pain.

(21) **Psalm 23:4**
Even though I walk through the valley of the
shadow of death, I will fear no evil, for you
are with me; your rod and your staff, they
comfort me.

The word *phantom*, in this case, doesn't mean that the pain is an apparition or a figment of one's imagination. In medical terms, it refers to the place where your mind believes the pain is originating. As I lay in bed, my left arm, although gone, felt as if it were resting in my lap. I could feel my wrist and forearm making contact with the sheet, and my hand felt as if it were clamped into a fist, clutching ever more tightly onto a ball of fire, while my fingertips buried themselves into my palm so that I thought they would come out the back of my hand. Of course, none of this could be real. It wasn't until I made eye contact with my amputation that my brain could pinpoint the location of the pain, at which time the pain would relocate to inside the remaining portion of my arm. This only served to intensify the pain, because now my hand/fist felt trapped inside the stump, producing a kind of claustrophobic feeling. The strange part was that the whole process would begin anew the moment

I looked away. The entire effect was brought on by angry nerve endings that had been violently and abruptly severed. This ghostly condition could persist for weeks and months—and from my understanding, even years. Amazingly, though, my need to tell of the greatness of God as it related to the accident superseded my tremendous discomfort. The Lord had left an indelible mark upon my heart that I would use as my guide to tell this story—a story that would glorify the Father and praise His Son. A reminder to believers and unbelievers alike of the power and compassion of the Lord our God.

And so it was this that I had in the forethoughts of my mind when my brother Jeff and his wife, Rita, arrived that Saturday afternoon for a visit (their second visit, the first being while I was asleep). The physical presence and natural strength of my brother, older and closest to me in age, brought another dimension to my circumstance. My brother and I had never been overly close. His interests and mine rarely intersected, yet I found my willingness to lean into him for support was total and without hesitation. I expressed a few sentiments and my brother nodded, but it wasn't long before we were both brought to tears. Tears that spoke of lost opportunities on both of our parts.

Jeff's being a veterinarian didn't preclude him from recognizing and diagnosing the problem I had developed in my feet and lower legs. They were swollen with fluid, retained from too many days of lying in bed. As he massaged the fluid back into the tissue, I related to him and Rita some of the details of the accident, revealing for the first time to anyone that my experience with the Holy Spirit had instilled in me a feeling of freedom— like the chains of this world had been thrown off. In fact, I had been released from bondage. (22) I finished by saying that Jesus is the King of kings and the Lord of hosts. If they were surprised by my choice of words, they couldn't have been more surprised than I. More prophetic words have never been spoken—at least, not by me.

(22) **John 14:6**

Jesus answered, "I am the way and the truth
and the life.
No one comes to the Father except through me."

As a Christian, these terms that I used to describe the God of all creation were not unknown to me, but they were not really part of my lexicon. To utter these phrases is to invoke a certain "knowing" that God is sovereign. He is the beginning, middle, and end of everything. (23) My faith had taken on a new shape. You might say it was transformed from a resignation to God's authority to a declaration of His authority. It may sound like semantics, but the difference lies in the joy and adulation in which each is stated. Furthermore, resignation to God's authority often occupies space in one's mind, while the declaration of God's authority occupies space in one's heart.

(23) **Psalm 90:1-2**
Lord, you have been our dwelling place
throughout all generations.
Before the mountains were born or before
you brought forth the whole world,
from everlasting to everlasting you are God.

The visit concluded with my hapless effort to drink an A&W root beer that I had requested they bring. My swallow problem prohibited me from sipping it. We brainstormed on how to deliver at least its taste. We soaked the root beer on a sponge designed to swab a dry mouth. I was unable to hold the sponge, so Rita volunteered to help. Our idea of root beer on a sponge worked, but it didn't produce the enjoyment I had hoped for, so we abandoned our efforts. The whole root beer experience served as a precursor to the helplessness I would have to endure for the foreseeable future.

* * *

I was truly incapacitated. I didn't know how long my need for help with every facet of life would last. So, with the Lord's guidance, I decided to embrace my less-than-vigorous vitality. Of course, I didn't accept my condition in the long term, but for now, I would make every effort to be cheerful rather than grumpy. I leave it to others to judge whether or not I accomplished my goal.

The trauma of the accident and the many hours sedated while in surgery had rendered my body more or less useless. I literally couldn't lift my head off the pillow. My legs were like noodles, even though they hadn't been affected by the spinal cord injury, leaving the bed pan as my best option for the bathroom. In addition, I had developed a rash from the pain medications, which had me feeling like I had rolled around in a field of nettles. The oxygen I was on had dried my nose, making it feel like a piece of dehydrated fruit left to bake in the sun after having fallen off the back of a delivery truck while driving through a desert. The bed was so uncomfortable, I was convinced of a conspiracy purposefully making it so that no one would want to stay in the hospital one second longer than need be. I had always been a side sleeper, but now, due to my injuries, I was forced to lie on my back, hour after interminable hour. Then, to top it off, I was informed at the end of my first day on the fourth floor that I would need to have the catheter reinserted.

To that end, a nurse practitioner (NP) arrived in the early evening to replace the catheter that had been removed in the TLC. Kelly and I tried to explain that I had

had an injury at the time of my first catheterization in the ER, and that we thought it best to have a doctor of urology perform the procedure. Well, she would hear none of it. She quickly informed us of her qualifications. She further emphasized that she had inserted many catheters during her time as a nurse practitioner and saw no reason why this time should prove to be her undoing. As a magnanimous gesture, she allowed me one last attempt to "go" on my own. Kelly and I thought her abruptness unsettling but were too new at this hospital thing to stand by our convictions. Having been informed that I was unable to "go" on my own, the NP returned, and the procedure got underway. After about fifteen minutes and a lot of aggravation and discomfort on my part, she exited the room and called for a doctor of urology. The doctor had the job done in a couple of minutes after her arrival. I never saw that nurse practitioner again, whom I now, jokingly, refer to as "Nurse Ratched"—the not-so-nice nurse popularized in the movie *One Flew Over the Cuckoo's Nest*. I'll never know with certainty what made her so unpleasant. Maybe she was just having a bad day. If that was the case, I surely could relate. In any event, the Bible reminds us that we will encounter difficult people from time to time.

As the week on the fourth floor unfolded, it became increasingly clear that the staff's main objective was to deprive me of sleep. At least, that truth seemed apparent in my mind. Thank God I had Kelly and at times, my sister Jackie, to run interference when my eyelids were too heavy to keep open. The mornings started around 6:00 a.m., with the first of many appearances of a certified nursing assistant to collect vital signs. The procedure didn't always require me to be awake, but often their entering the room was just enough to make me stir—especially since my slumber was very shallow.

On one occasion, a pharmacy technician politely knocked and came into my room. He wanted to know if I wanted a flu shot. It was just after 4:30 in the morning, and Kelly, who had stayed overnight, got to him before he got to me. She answered for me in a whisper by saying, "He probably doesn't want one, especially since he's never seen the need for one before." She then showed the tech to the door. She muttered something about "the time of morning" as she got back onto the cot the staff had set up for her. The intrusion wasn't very long, but it created just enough commotion to wake me.

The sandman and I were becoming reacquainted just about the time the nursing assistant came through the door to get my vital signs. It was 6:00 a.m. Like it or not, unless I could sneak in a nap, I was up for the day.

Plastics would appear each morning between 6 and 7 o'clock to change the dressing on my arm. The doctors from plastics would quietly enter my room each morning and flash an apologetic smile, as if asking forgiveness for the earliness of their call. Very little was said between us—good morning and thank you was the extent of my end of the conservation. The healing process was right on track, so I'm sure the doctor in charge saw no need for a detailed question and answer session. She worked so quickly and efficiently that one couldn't help but notice how skilled she was at her craft. In a few minutes, I had a fresh bandage. Then she and her team would leave as quickly as they had arrived, turning the light off as they left in the hope that I might get a little more rest before the nurses' shift change.

It was on the first of these occasions that I had a sustained look at my stump. I remembered looking at it in the field, but of course, that was an obstructed view, covered in part by the bloodied and torn coat sleeve. This viewing was entirely different. It was a messy sight, to say the least. It was extremely red, and crisscrossed with stitches where the muscle and skin had been sewn over the bone. There was a large open wound on the bicep. Through the natural healing process, this would close itself over the next eight months. The most distinguishing feature, however, was the swelling. It was swollen to nearly three times its normal size. It wasn't distressing to look at during these dressing changes. In fact, these viewings helped to add another level of acceptance.

The nurses' shift change happened at 7:00 a.m. As attentive as they were, a patient couldn't expect much help at this time of morning. Fortunately, I was never alone. I always had Kelly or Jackie to fill in the gaps. The nurses seemed to appreciate them. If they didn't, they never let on. If the other patients on the fourth floor had seen the way that my wife and sister waited on me, they would have thought me spoiled. Indeed, they would have been correct in their assumption. I learned from the staff that all too often, patients in their care had little to no support from family or friends. Luckily for me, that wasn't the case. Being from a large family and having a wide circle of friends was a real advantage. By mid-week, the calls, cards, and visitors started to pour in. Soon, the walls of my hospital room were covered in get well cards. I found the sentiments expressed on them quite wonderful. Although the cards that actually had the words "Get Well" amused me. Since my arm was never going to grow back, I didn't envision myself "getting well"; "getting by" in my new condition seemed more likely. Nonetheless, I took great comfort in knowing that so many wished me well.

While my desire to receive visitors was expanding, my need for better rest continued unabated. A nurse with great instincts could see my dilemma and had mercy on me. With the exception of plastics, she found a way to consolidate my cares, which resulted in fewer interruptions from the staff. The energy I would need to begin to tell others of the glory of God was found. It was an answer to a prayer.

One of the greatest actions a Christian can take is to be a witness for Christ Jesus. (24) The Holy Spirit had invigorated me to do just that. As visitors arrived, I could see in their faces a pre-conception—one that questioned what they may encounter in someone who had suffered such a permanent loss. Seeing someone in my broken condition is often the last thing people want to do. To their credit, they overcame their hesitations. Their words sounded strong and encouraging, but the pain and concern on their faces betrayed them. My heart really went out to them. As for me, I was extremely weak in body, but I had never been stronger in Spirit. (25) I would often try to put them at ease using humor—sometimes by saying, "Rumors of my death have been greatly exaggerated." Still other times, I would simply express my gratitude to them for coming.

(24) **Matthew 10:32**
"Whoever acknowledges me before others,
I will also acknowledge before my Father
in heaven."

(25) **2 Corinthians 12:9**
But he said to me, "My grace is sufficient
for you, for my power is made perfect in
weakness."

My friends and family encompass a broad spectrum. So, when they heard my story, it elicited many different responses. Some cried at having their faith reinforced—possibly because my story was the most tangible evidence they'd ever experienced of their long-held belief in God. Others listened in quiet wonderment—their attention sustained throughout. And some, finding the story incredible, seemed distracted and would often look away. They may have been debating who was doing the talking—me, or the pain medication.

However, some of the most unique reactions came from the nursing staff, both at the regular hospital, then later at the UW Rehab Hospital. Dealing with serious illness and traumatic injury is a daily occurrence for them. The patients in their care will experience varying degrees of recovery. I can't even imagine the difficulty these caregivers must have in coping with what they see. It must be, at times, a heavy load to carry. The nurses, as individuals, were amazingly strong and highly reasoned people. I was astounded at the way their craft and faith seemed to be interwoven. Both of these ideals were like separate patches on the same quilt. As caregivers, their desire to know that God could unburden them of their daily pressures was the common thread that ran between these two principles.

The phantom pain continued unceasingly, interrupted only by the next push of the pain pump. The sensation that my missing hand was opening and closing at will was new and somewhat distracting. Interruptions from staff were far fewer now, allowing for more catnaps, but deep sleep still remained elusive. In my estimation, I was taking every discomfort in stride except one. My unending complaint about the NG-tube prompted a visit from the speech therapist—the same one who had conducted the formal swallow test. She conducted a bedside test and found that I had improved enough to be allowed a pureed diet. In other words, a diet with the consistency of baby food. It didn't sound very appetizing, but I was elated, because I thought this meant the immediate removal of the NG-tube. I couldn't have been more wrong. I was informed by the hospital nutritionist that I would need to consume, by mouth, upwards of 2,500 calories a day before the feeding tube would be removed. I was highly motivated and set out on a course to accomplish this goal. Although it proved to be easier said than done.

Dietary brought a menu from which I ordered spaghetti, garlic bread, sweet corn, and pears for dessert. In my mind's eye, I envisioned a grand meal coming my way, and so I looked forward with great anticipation for supper to arrive. I was like a kid waiting for Christmas. Suppertime couldn't come soon enough. Just about the time I was ready to burst, room service came through the door. A CNA moved the bed to an upright position, placed the tray in front of me, and removed its cover. It smelled good, but lacked eye appeal. Everything I had ordered was there, except the garlic bread. I guess the kitchen couldn't figure out how to puree bread. The moment of truth had arrived. Since I was unable to hold a utensil, Kelly helped spoon feed me. I took a couple of tenuous bites. I'm happy to say, it tasted pretty good. It was the texture that had me wondering how I was going to eat 2,000 plus calories of this "goo" every day! With the only alternative being the NG-tube, I miraculously found the stomach for this requirement. In three days, the NG-tube was pulled. It was a not-so-small victory, and a big reason to celebrate.

From my hospital bed on the fourth floor, I could hear the Flight-For-Life helicopter arriving several times each day, bringing critical care patients and on occasion, donor organs. It always made me sorrowful, thinking about the troubled souls aboard it. I was listening to one of these flights landing late in the week when an occupational therapist (OT) bounded through my door. She was young and full of energy and determined to address my most urgent need. The spinal cord injury had left my right arm and hand with diminished capabilities. My biceps were strong, but my triceps' ability was almost nonexistent. In fact, one occasion stands out. I had an itch on my nose, and I raised my hand toward my face to scratch. At its apex my arm, from elbow to fingertips, just hinged together and fell with a thud next to my head on the pillow. I shouldered my arm back to a resting position beside me. Not knowing what to make of this occurrence, I lay there in a moment of silence while I took inventory of my predicament.

However, the challenges with my hand were not unknown, like that of my triceps. I was unable to open and extend my fingers and thumb. I had lost the sense of touch, while a numb and tingly sensation persisted. Being "balled into a fist" had become my hand's favored position.

The occupational therapist took my arm into her hands. She conducted a few tests, obtaining some strength and flexibility measurements. In about twenty minutes, she decided upon a course of action. She would build a splint that would use a series of rubber bands to pull open my fingers, and as a by-product of that effort, my entire hand would be held open. I said, "I find the idea intriguing, because through the years, I have had to come up with creative ideas on the farm to solve one problem or another." We mused for a moment, wondering if OTs and farmers may have more in common than one might imagine. As she left, I said, "I wish I could have been more helpful, but I'm a little short-handed at the moment." I had already ascertained that she had a witty personality, but she turned back with a perplexed look on her face. I smiled broadly and then she, having made the connection, smiled back, acknowledging my attempt at humor. (26)

(26) **Proverbs 17:22**
A cheerful heart is good medicine.

PART THREE

Rehab Hospital

Saturday morning dawned clear and cold. It was November 10. I learned then that my twelve-day stay at the UW Hospital was over, and I would be transferred to the UW Rehab Hospital between 10 and 11 o'clock that morning. Kelly immediately set about the task of packing up my personal effects. There wasn't a lot, since my life here had been limited. The bulk of the job consisted of peeling the greeting cards off the walls and boxing them up, so they could be transferred to my new home. I thought about how these "get well" cards could have been "sympathy" cards if the Lord had willed a different outcome. It wasn't a chilling thought; it was simply the acknowledgement of a truth. My nurse swung into action, preparing discharge papers and readying me for transport. Since we weren't exactly sure when the transport vehicle would arrive, we hurried, making the process feel rushed. It turned out to be one of those hurry-up-and-wait situations. Eventually, the driver arrived, with apologies for her tardiness, but made no mention of the reason for delay. She rapidly positioned the wheelchair next to the bed and set the brakes. My nurse and Kelly helped me to be seated. Then the transport driver took control and rolled me down the hallway toward the elevators. I left with thumbs up and encouraging words from the staff on the fourth floor as I, in return, expressed words of gratitude and goodbyes. It was difficult to leave, but it was time.

When we exited the hospital into the drive-up, the cold air was a shock, especially given that I'd been living in a very warm environment for almost two weeks. It was good to feel the crisp late autumn air on my face. Not knowing what to expect, I was surprised when our lady escort used a winch to pull the wheelchair into the back of the van. This method provided a smooth and steady pull, rather than the herky-jerky motion that manually pushing the chair up the ramp may have produced. Also, our driver was a little-bitty thing that may have found it beyond her ability to push larger patients. Within moments, she had me safely belted into the wheelchair and had secured the chair itself to the floor. Then off we went.

Kelly sat up front and made small talk with the driver for the twenty-five-minute sprint across town. We learned that she had come to the United States a few months before and had already purchased this medical transportation service. Though here only a short while, she drove with confidence on the streets of Madison like it was her native city.

The Lord provided us safe travel, and by early afternoon, I was settled into my new room in this two-story, forty-bed rehab facility. The room itself was more spacious and less cluttered than the room at the UW Hospital, but much to my chagrin, the bed was every bit as uncomfortable. The admissions nurse came by and checked me in while Kelly made calls, informing family and friends of our move. Having finished the paperwork, the admissions nurse told me that my therapy would begin Monday, and for now, my diet would stay the same. So, other than receiving my meds, I was free for the remainder of Saturday and all of Sunday.

Kelly pulled a chair close to the bed and clicked on the TV. This was the first time I had viewed TV since the accident. There was a college football game on, but it didn't hold my interest, and soon, Kelly turned it off. The ride from the hospital and the cold air had thoroughly worn me out. I rested my eyes while Kelly held my forearm and prayed in Jesus' name for my rest and relief. (27)

(27) **Exodus 33:14**
"My presence will go with you, and I will give you rest."

Jackie brought Ethan by on Sunday afternoon so we could watch the Green Bay Packers game. I explained to Jackie how uncomfortable the bed was, so she thought it might be helpful to flip the mattress. Kelly and Ethan put the gait belt on me and assisted me into a chair. The second my weight came off the bed it triggered an alarm at the nurses' station, which brought a nurse to my room on the fly. We learned that the hospital bed was equipped with a safety device that alerts a nurse to the possibility that a patient has fallen out of bed. The nurse sternly, yet gently, advised us not to make a move like that again without her help. We all felt a little embarrassed as we promised to do as she asked. In the end, the mattress got turned, and it made a big difference.

Late in the day, Pastor Dave and his wife stopped by for a very welcome visit. They brought along with them another couple from our church. They all had seen me at my worst and were somewhat taken aback at the speed of my recovery. I could do nothing but agree, for I felt much stronger. That first weekend spent at the rehab hospital had me feeling like I'd turned a corner. And even though the work of rehab would wear me thin at times, never would I relinquish any gains I'd made, no matter how small.

Monday morning presented a brand-new face to my hospitalization. Gone were the vital signs monitors, the abundant in-room visits from nurses and physicians, and all the time spent solely in bed, secluded from other patients. Lost, also, was the impulse to reach for things with my left hand. I was surprised how quickly this natural instinct of fifty-three years deserted me. Of course, there were traces of the old routine. I would see the attending physician each morning, and my dressing would still be changed twice daily. And, naturally, I still needed help with my catheter and pain meds. That's where the similarities ended. Here at the rehab hospital, I would have caregivers with completely different skill sets, and I would meet patients with many different maladies. I would be out of my room for therapy for three hours per day, plus walks in the hallways whenever there was someone to accompany me. In addition, I was encouraged to take my meals in the cafeteria. In a broader sense, a lot would be expected of me during my two-week stay at the rehab hospital. The Lord definitely had me feeling up to the challenge. (28)

(28) **Isaiah 41:10**
"So do not fear, for I am with you; do not be dismayed, for I am your God.
I will strengthen you and help you;
I will uphold you with my righteous right hand."

My diet had been upgraded from pureed to diced and chopped, which made mealtime something to look forward to again, even though swallowing remained difficult. Despite all of the unfavorable things I'd heard about hospital food, I discovered this wasn't always the case. In fact, I never had a bad meal in rehab. The patients were offered breakfast, dinner, and supper—and in my case, all the snacks I wanted in between meals, and sometimes snacks I didn't want, in an effort to help me reach the goal of 2,500 calories per day. I started to long for the days when I would be allowed to stop eating after I was full. To coin a phrase—and use it as it wasn't intended—"my cup runneth over."

During the first week, a CNA would transport me to the cafeteria in a wheelchair. The gait belt was always fitted around me before I ventured away from the bed. It wasn't long before my unasked question of "Why do I need this belt?" was answered. In my zeal to get moving during one of these transfers from bed to wheelchair, I lost my balance and was quickly righted by the CNA using a firm grip on the belt. I was glad that I had never wondered aloud about the procedural use of the gait belt. As with our Heavenly Father's commands, certain rules are best for us, even when we don't see the need. (29)

(29) **John 14:23**
Jesus replied, "Anyone who loves me will obey
my teaching. My Father will love them, and
we will come to them and make our home
with them."

On the schedule after breakfast, there was usually a
consultation in my room with the attending physician. I
found him a bit of an automaton, but likeable, and since
my concerns were few, these visits were short. After that
came physical therapy (PT). My initial meeting with the
PT was on the first Monday after my admittance. The
PT assigned to my case exuded a calm and confident de-
meanor and spoke with a quiet self-assuredness. I had
an immediate liking for her. Directly, and without any
hint of pretense, she asked, "What is most important
to you going forward?" I hadn't given the future much
thought, but my answer came quickly. I said, "I want to
be useful in the home." She replied, "Well then, let's get
started." She helped me into the wheelchair, placed the
catheter bag onto my lap, and off we went to the gym.

For the first week in rehab, I always went to and fro
in the chair. I sometimes cracked the joke that the staff
liked to push me around. Of course, they'd heard that
one a million times, but they always humored me with
a faint chuckle. When we arrived at the gym, the PT

wheeled me toward a corner at the far end. As I rolled along, I got a good look at the equipment. There were balls, balloons, ropes, pulleys, stair steps to climb, patients seated around tables playing board games, and multi-colored objects that at first glance looked like giant rubber bands. There was even what appeared to be a life-sized toy car in the opposite corner. For all intents and purposes, it gave the appearance of a playground designed for three-year-olds. Of course, there were some pieces of equipment that were much more sophisticated, of which I had no idea of their functions. The fact is, at this early stage in my rehab, I didn't recognize that this space was uniquely developed for people with broken bodies to regain a semblance of independence.

Having reached our destination, the PT locked my wheelchair brakes and explained the series of walking exercises she expected me to attempt. She would use these maneuvers to assess my balance. The PT walked alongside me while I performed the routine, which proved to be well-advised given my instability. Once completed, I returned to my chair while the PT added up the numbers. I had scored a 14 out of a possible 30. I knew going in that I wasn't ready to run a marathon, but still, I was a little surprised at my poor performance. It was all too obvious that I had a lot of work to do before they would consider it safe for me to go home. As we went back to my room, I was determined to do better tomorrow. And with the Lord's help, I knew I would.

Later that morning was OT. While PT was designed to get me on my feet again, OT was designed to help me learn techniques so I could live with my disability. My OT was rigid and somewhat abrasive, but always had my best interest at heart. She was a real taskmaster and proved to be just what I needed for the road ahead. Her focus was on "everyday" chores such as shaving, showering, dental care, feeding, and dressing myself. These were considerable challenges, given the fact that my remaining arm was functioning at about 25 percent or less of its normal capabilities. My OT said it was important to reestablish my arm and hand's memory of their many uses. This is to say that I was to take an active role in my recovery, rather than the wait-and-see approach.

Throughout my time at the rehab hospital she put me through the paces, using many exercises intended to restore function. Some were very painful, but gains were definitely made in the two weeks under her care and guidance. Yet just as often, we discovered that the simple act of attempting routine, daily chores was equally helpful. My ability to perform ordinary tasks that I used to take for granted bordered on the ridiculous. Things such as repeatedly dropping eating utensils, eye glasses, toothbrushes, shaving razors, and the remote control; repositioning a pillow, dressing/undressing (in particular, putting on socks); lacking the strength for every personal need in the bathroom; and ending with my favorite: applying shaving cream with the backs of my fingers. All of these things and more—in juxtaposition to the one-time fence building, firewood cutting, machinery repairing, hay baling, cattle and crop raising, roofing and building, jack-of-all-trades that I used to be—was occasionally, in a very strange sort of way, very funny. The Lord had undeniably instilled in me a sense of humor for this situation. A sense of humor that has been helpful ever since.

My own recovery notwithstanding, God had perfectly placed me where he needed me to be. The patients I encountered in rehab suffered from a variety of afflictions such as heart disease, strokes, brain disorders, and amputations due to diabetes and accidents, to name a few. Yet our common bond was that we all had been dealt a crushing blow to our state of being due to a sudden change in our physical capabilities. And so, I could think of no better place to be a witness for the Lord. At the same time, I realized that I had a captive audience, so in presentation, I treaded lightly. Those who were firm in their faith welcomed my story with tremendous enthusiasm. Others were less convinced of God but always exhibited an eagerness to hear. Still others demonstrated a more obvious need to hear the Good News.

Oddly enough, it wasn't a fellow patient, but a nurse that I met near the end of my stay in rehab who had the strongest reaction. She arrived in my room shortly after I had pushed the nurses' call station button for assistance. She entered with a smile and explained that my assigned nurse was busy, and then asked how she could help. I, rather apologetically, told her that my pillows had slipped and I was unable to readjust them, and that I was sorry to bother her for something so trivial. She responded by saying, "It's all part of the job." She got me repositioned and then asked how I came to be in rehab. Among other things, I told her that I had had a wonderful life on a small farm, punctuated by one terrible mistake. She must have gleaned from our conversation that I wasn't distressed, because she commented that my disposition seemed remarkable and that my positive attitude would serve me well. I made plain that I attributed my outlook to the strength given me by my Lord and Savior, Jesus Christ. The tears streamed down her face as I related how the Holy Spirit had enveloped me as I prayed in Jesus' name. She then revealed that her once-strong faith had been eroded away little by little by the trials of daily life. I encouraged her to seek God once again. She said she wasn't exactly sure how to go about that and rapidly regained her professional composure. That conversation will always be a reminder to me to be gentle, but not timid, in witnessing for the Lord. (30) And I pray that hearing the Good News again, as demonstrated through my story, will start her on a path back to Jesus.

(30) **2 Timothy 1:7**
"For God did not give us a spirit of timidity,
but a spirit of power, of love and of
self-discipline."

The second and far more successful walking/stability test, in which I now scored 27 out of 30, signaled that my time at the rehab hospital was drawing to a close. I would be going home soon, but not before receiving the highly sought after but rarely bestowed green bracelet, signifying that the patient was allowed to walk in the hallways without an assistant. It was both a small step forward and a big achievement. My efforts in PT produced a quick and fruitful outcome, which was expected. My progress in OT was less so, which was not entirely unexpected. At any rate, OT would continue in an outpatient setting for months to come.

That coming Sunday, I was released. Kelly boxed up my belongings and pulled down the get-well cards. Their numbers had grown considerably during my two-week stay. Their removal made the room seem very barren. Naturally, I had some uneasiness about losing all the care and support I had been receiving. Still, I knew it was time to leave. I said goodbye to as many caregivers as I could as we made our way to the car. As Kelly buckled my seatbelt, I quipped that we'd spent a month in Madison but hadn't seen any of the sights or attractions. With that small attempt at humor, Kelly started the car, slowly pulled out of the circle drive-up, and headed for home.

PART FOUR

Home

The forty-five-minute journey home was a quiet one. Kelly and I held hands and chit-chatted a bit, but primarily we were silent, as our thoughts led us both to the same conclusion: that if the accident, care, and recovery had turned out differently, this ride would not be happening. And so we drove on in solemn gratitude, quickly leaving the city behind. As we advanced into the countryside, we moved past harvested fields of corn and soybeans, but also spotted many unharvested fields, for the fall had been cold and wet, delaying the farmers' progress. (31) As we got closer to home, more familiar sights came into view. The landscape as well as neighbors' homes and outbuildings were all unchanged, as I knew they would be.

(31) James 5:7
"Be patient, then, brothers and sisters, until the Lord's coming. See how the farmer waits for the land to yield its valuable crop, patiently waiting for the autumn and spring rains."

The route took us past the accident site. The location itself held no particular meaning for me. Gone was the harvesting equipment that had been there a month earlier. The tractor and corn picker had been returned to and parked in our farmyard. I gave a passing thought to my spilled blood that I was sure, by now, had been washed away by the rain and snow. The fact that part of my body had returned to the earth was of no significance. Rather, it was the blood of Jesus, shed on the cross for my salvation, that filled my thoughts as we drove past. (32)

(32) **Matthew 26:28**
"This is my blood of the covenant,
which is poured out for many for the forgiveness of sins."

Just past the accident site was Mom and Dad's house. We stopped for a brief visit. We pulled up to the garage door and parked. Kelly came around, unbuckled the seat belt, and helped me out of the car. As Kelly held my right arm, we paused a moment, and I mentally measured the distance between Mom and Dad's house and the cornfield where I was injured. The idea that my call for help could bridge that distance under the best of circumstances was understandable, but the adverse conditions that had existed that day reaffirmed the "knowing" that God had put my voice in Mom's ear.

Kelly and I turned toward the house. By then, Ethan had come to greet us, and we all went inside together. I embraced Mom at the door and then sat next to Dad at the kitchen table. It was somewhat difficult to face Dad, because he had always advised me, in earnest, to be very careful around machinery. Yet at the age of eighty-nine, he was all too aware of how fast reversals of fortune can happen. I took heart in knowing that it gave him tremendous relief to see that I was on the mend. Our short stay concluded, as we all came to the predominantly unspoken understanding that even though life had undergone a big change, everything was going to be okay. It was an awareness that my parents not only needed, but more importantly, deserved. We left Mom and Dad's with Ethan in tow, and in two or three minutes, we were home.

Since I harbored no obsession with and had no intention of scrutinizing the machine that took my arm and broke my neck, my first act of being home caught me off guard. As we entered the yard, the corn picker parked nearby came into view, and I couldn't resist the natural urge to take a closer look. Kelly drove over to it and parked. Together, we walked along its right side. I peered into the compartment which housed the chain, gear, and shaft that had held me in its grip. No fragments remained of my arm or coat. The same cousin who had returned the tractor and picker weeks before had, to his credit, undertaken the unenviable task of cutting loose and removing the coat sleeve and my arm that was crushed inside. I am loath to single out any one person for the many acts of kindness I received during this entire experience, but I do maintain the utmost appreciation for this one. (33) On the whole, the scene standing by the picker held little physical or emotional interest, and as we returned to the car, I gave glory to God for sparing me any fixation one might have had on this inanimate object.

(33) **2 Samuel 2:6**
"May the Lord now show you kindness
and faithfulness,
and I too will show you the same favor because you have done this."

Kelly, Ethan, and I drove the short distance from the machinery lot to the house, thus ending my longest-ever time away from home. With a less-than-solid grasp on the newly installed handrail, I made my way up the steps and in through the front door. For a farmer, it can be difficult to describe the meaning of home. I've been at home in the field, the wood, and the barn, but those are places of labor. Knowing that those aforementioned places were now of far less value to me made this a homecoming like no other.

The house was warm and inviting on this cold, late November day. Jackie had installed handrails and grab bars both inside and out, and Kelly had made other small changes to accommodate her now disabled husband. Together we would decide what, if any, bigger changes had to be made in the future. Kelly got me settled into a chair and asked if I was hungry. I replied, "Yes, I'm starved." She then brought me a large plateful of macaroni and cheese for lunch. Much to my wonderment, I overate. The very thing I had pledged, in rehab, not to do again. Evidently, the all-you-can-eat diet that I'd had in the hospital had followed me home. To say it bluntly, I simply wanted comfort foods in all their forms.

Mom and Dad and some friends came by to celebrate Ethan's birthday the following afternoon. A few cattle still remained, and Ethan attended to them before the party. It was quite a sight to behold my newly-turned twelve-year-old son outfitted in my old, worn chore coat. It was too big, but he wore it with confidence and—dare I say—pride, derived out of his recent promotion as the "go-to-man" on the farm.

The months of December and January zipped past, and with them the holiday season. Christmas was highlighted with the opportunity to witness for the Lord to our church congregation, and New Year's Day came and went with the usual sense of optimism. My apprehensions about having enough support at home were allayed. Kelly was essentially pulling double duty, with combined efforts at home and at her job. Ethan was quick to help at every turn, and family and friends offered support for our every possible need. My days were filled with short walks bracketed by Kelly and Ethan, a steady stream of visitors, attempts at small chores around the house, going to the barn with Ethan at chore time to lend him moral support, twice daily dressing changes on my stump—as I had opted for natural healing, rather than a skin graft, therapy, doctors' follow-up appointments, and enormous amounts of rest.

As to the visitors I received, there were so very many. Along with them came an abundance of questions. The bulk of them were inquiries such as, "How are you feeling? How's the pain? Are you glad to be home? Is there anything you need?"

Other questions rose to the next level of curiosity. Mainly, "How did the accident happen?" I described for them the events leading up to, during, and directly after being caught in the corn picker. Having already deduced how an incident like mine usually occurs, they were quickly satisfied with my response. However, these questions seemed only to scratch the surface of that which was really wanting to be known. To that end, the most common and probing question was "What will become of the farm now?"

Rather than deflect or evade this question, I welcomed it, for the Lord had prepared me well on how to answer. I expressed to them that all the furnishings of this property, such as fences, machinery, structures, livestock, and any hope and trust I had placed in them, were all in time, destined to fall down, die, and decay. I knew that through His infinite mercies, God had re-positioned Himself well in front of any earthly aspirations that I might think important. I pray that all those that received that answer would find it applicable as a means of peace in their own lives. I know I have. (34)

(34) **Micah 5:13**
"I will destroy your idols and your sacred
stones from among you;
you will no longer bow down to the work of
your hands.

In February, I made arrangements to meet with the emergency room staff at the Fort Atkinson hospital, the first link in the healthcare chain to assist in my recovery. Kelly and I wanted to extend our gratitude to them. I contacted the director of ER services to ask if a meeting could be permitted. She said it was somewhat rare, but she was excited at the idea and would get back to me about a possible date and time. Two days later I had my answer. She had scheduled a get-together for February 17 at 7:30 a.m. The two-week wait for our visit went by in a flash. From the time I came home from the hospital, time seemed to elapse rapidly. Days were like hours, hours like minutes. And so, the morning of the visit was upon us before we knew it.

Kelly and I arrived a little early and were escorted to a conference room near the ER. Minutes later the room was full. We were amazed to learn that there had been fourteen people involved in my care, twelve of whom were in attendance. It was definitely an emotionally charged scene. After introductions, I began to relate to them the cause of my injuries and the story surrounding it—I hadn't intended to, but it seemed only natural to let them know how it was that I came to be in their care. When I told them of the peace and calm that I had received from the Holy Spirit as I prayed the 23rd Psalm, tears filled all of our eyes. It tends to be the part of the story that has the greatest impact.

When next I spoke, I imparted to them that when I was in their ER I remembered a lot of movement around me, but that I couldn't remember anyone's face. Yet there had been one voice besides my wife's that had echoed in my mind ever since. And so I asked, "Is the person here today who said in answer to my question about my shoulder, 'Yes, I think you'll keep your shoulder'?" Shortly, there came a nod in response from a nurse who had been on duty the morning I was brought in. I told her of the quieting effect that her voice and words had on me, and I tried to verbalize my appreciation for her but struggled to find the words. I hope the tears that filled my eyes were enough to let her know how much those seven words she spoke had meant. That nurse's reply to me that morning in the ER wasn't just another one of the many moments that shaped the outcome of the accident. Instead, it was an answer from God to a specific question for my need to know what was remaining of my arm. I know the Holy Spirit spoke through her. (35)

(35) **Psalm 102:1-2**
Hear my prayer, Lord;
let my cry for help come to you.
Do not hide your face from me
when I am in distress.
Turn your ear to me; when I call,
answer me quickly.

It also came to light by several individuals that I had prayed aloud. More specifically, they said that I had prayed for them as caregivers. I said, "I remember exactly what I prayed for you. I asked God to give you strength and to help you draw on your knowledge." Not all, but most, recollected that prayer. I had been slightly concerned that maybe I had rambled on, disrupting their efforts. So I asked, "Would you rather I had been quiet so you could better attend to me?" They replied with a resounding, "No, those words really helped us to calm down and focus."

With some reluctance on the part of everyone, the gathering came to an end. It had been an amazing event with a hint of nostalgia—like a reunion of long-ago classmates—and the ease of being together, born out of familiarity and linked, in this case, by the memory of a single event. The assembly culminated with hugs from both Kelly and myself at the door as these gifted and committed gatekeepers of other people's wellbeing filed past.

We continued in conversation with that same special nurse at the entryway to the ER. When the topic turned to the upcoming fair and Ethan's 4-H project, it sparked in Kelly and me a new claim on normalcy—a sensation we'd been without for over three months. As we stepped into the open air of the parking lot, Kelly and I recognized that remnants of our old life still existed, but we also knew that God had placed us on a different course, and we would walk this new path with faith, letting Him lead the way. (36)

(36) Proverbs 3:6
In all your ways submit to him, and he will make your paths straight.

Epilogue

The passage of time lends itself to retrospection. The calendar year has flipped since the day of the accident. Neighbors have all but completed another harvest. My only participation was that of spectator. At the one-year check-up, the surgeon who repaired my neck reviewed the new x-ray and surmised the three most possible scenarios my injuries could have produced. The first, and most obvious: the life I'm currently living. The second: paralysis from the neck down. And the third: death. There's no doubt that in the physical realm, the second and third alternatives surely exist, but I reject them both as little more than the good doctors' vast knowledge of how the body works. As a Christian, I believe that God knows my life from beginning to end. Certainly, there are choices we make, but none are made without God's foreknowledge. The comfort derived from this part of faith is immeasurable and puts the Christian in a great position to weather life's storms. With that frame of reference, it's difficult to consider what happened as merely an accident. Of course, I know that God did not intend for me to be hurt this way. What happened was the natural result of sin in a fallen world. Consequences of sin manifest themselves in many ways. Our outright rebellion against our heavenly Father and the times that we don't fully trust in Him are two obstacles that keep us separated from Him.

At the risk of being too gory, this was a fairly slow-moving accident—unlike, for instance, a car accident that occurs fast and without control. The shaft my arm wrapped around was moving at a low rate of speed, leaving me with a number of seconds to think about my situation. I thought of turning the machine off, but that was impossible given my distance from the control lever. I then tried, unsuccessfully, to unzip my coat, hoping I could free myself by slipping my arm out of its sleeve. Both of these ideas failed as I continued to pull away with all my strength (trying to extract my arm with that much force is how the doctors believe I fractured and dislocated the vertebrae in my neck). I then cried out "No" three times. Most Christians know the scripture in the Gospels when Peter denied knowing the Lord three times, just as the Lord predicted he would. Of course, we know Peter was afraid of being identified as a disciple of Jesus, but it was also like he was declaring that he would be better off going it alone rather than admitting to knowing Jesus. Could it be any different for me?

I was searching for a way out. When I realized I could not free myself, I began to pray the 23rd Psalm—not for my life, but for God to be with me. And that's when I felt the Holy Spirit come upon me. The metaphor for trying to free myself from this machine and trying, in vain, to free myself from sin is a subtle but important part of this story that I hope is not lost on the reader.

While it can be said that I'm happy to be alive, I hope the larger part of this story conveys God's faithfulness to those who call upon Him in prayer and the rock-solid confidence that can be placed in Him, whatever the circumstance.

The challenges for me now are many. The vertebrae in my neck are secure but often leave me in a state of discomfort, and the nerves in my amputation burn without pause as I continue to pray that, with God, time or remedy will bring relief. The fingers on my right hand remain numb and tingly and don't fully open, while my right arm continues with a persistent weakness. I've begun the process of getting a left-arm prosthetic, but hold out no real hope that it might change my life in any meaningful way. In fact, with prayer, I guard against this world's wish list for fear that it might take me away from the all-consuming love of Jesus.

In its entirety, this event has left me in a relatively un-unique position. It's given me a deeper desire to serve God and advance His kingdom, while simultaneously, my need for the peace and security that only His Word can bring has grown. Both seemingly increasing equally. Yet of course, as a Christian, I know that these two positions held by the faithful can never be perfectly equal—the second will always exceed the first, which is why I rely solely on the one true God.

And so, I will continue to seek Him. For I know that which has been lost has been replaced with something far greater. The Lord Jesus' presence which surrounded me in that field will be with me forever. And while it may sound strange to some, I would never ask the return of two fully functioning arms if it meant forgetting the Lord's eternal promise that He will be with me whenever I humble myself and call upon Him by name. Then, with joy and adoration, elevate Him to His rightful place in my heart as Lord and Savior.

CPSIA information can be obtained
at www.ICGtesting.com
Printed in the USA
JSHW010157010822
28688JS00002B/10